Canadian Born

Canadian Born

E. Pauline Johnson

MINT EDITIONS

Canadian Born was first published in 1903.

This edition published by Mint Editions 2021.

ISBN 9781513223018 | E-ISBN 9781513221519

Published by Mint Editions®

MINT
EDITIONS

minteditionbooks.com

Publishing Director: Jennifer Newens
Design & Production: Rachel Lopez Metzger
Project Manager: Micaela Clark
Typesetting: Westchester Publishing Services

CONTENTS

Canadian Born

We first saw light in Canada, the land beloved of God;
We are the pulse of Canada, its marrow and its blood;
And we, the men of Canada, can face the world and brag
That we were born in Canada beneath the British flag.

Few of us have the blood of kings, few are of courtly birth,
But few are vagabonds or rogues of doubtful name and worth;
And all have one credential that entitles us to brag—
That we were born in Canada beneath the British flag.

We've yet to make our money, we've yet to make our fame,
But we have gold and glory in our clean colonial name;
And every man's a millionaire if only he can brag
That he was born in Canada beneath the British flag.

No title and no coronet is half so proudly worn
As that which we inherited as men Canadian born.
We count no man so noble as the one who makes the brag
That he was born in Canada beneath the British flag.

The Dutch may have their Holland, the Spaniard have his Spain,
The Yankee to the south of us must south of us remain;
For not a man dare lift a hand against the men who brag
That they were born in Canada beneath the British flag.

Where Leaps the Ste. Marie

I

What dream you in the night-time
    When you whisper to the moon?
What say you in the morning?
    What do you sing at noon?
When I hear your voice uplifting,
Like a breeze through branches sifting,
And your ripples softly drifting
    To the August airs a-tune.

II

Lend me your happy laughter,
    Ste. Marie, as you leap;
Your peace that follows after
    Where through the isles you creep.
Give to me your splendid dashing,
Give your sparkles and your splashing,
Your uphurling waves down crashing,
    Then, your aftermath of sleep.

Harvest Time

Pillowed and hushed on the silent plain,
Wrapped in her mantle of golden grain,

Wearied of pleasuring weeks away,
Summer is lying asleep today,—

Where winds come sweet from the wild-rose briers
And the smoke of the far-off prairie fires.

Yellow her hair as the goldenrod,
And brown her cheeks as the prairie sod;

Purple her eyes as the mists that dream
At the edge of some laggard sun-drowned stream;

But over their depths the lashes sweep,
For Summer is lying today asleep.

The north wind kisses her rosy mouth,
His rival frowns in the far-off south,

And comes caressing her sunburnt cheek,
And Summer awakes for one short week,—

Awakes and gathers her wealth of grain,
Then sleeps and dreams for a year again.

LADY LORGNETTE

I

Lady Lorgnette, of the lifted lash,
    The curling lip and the dainty nose,
The shell-like ear where the jewels flash,
    The arching brow and the languid pose,
The rare old lace and the subtle scents,
    The slender foot and the fingers frail,—
I may act till the world grows wild and tense,
    But never a flush on your features pale.
The footlights glimmer between us two,—
    You in the box and I on the boards,—
I am only an actor, Madame, to you,
    A mimic king 'mid his mimic lords,
For you are the belle of the smartest set,
        Lady Lorgnette.

II

Little Babette, with your eyes of jet,
    Your midnight hair and your piquant chin,
Your lips whose odors of violet
    Drive men to madness and saints to sin,—
I see you over the footlights' glare
    Down in the pit 'mid the common mob,—
Your throat is burning, and brown, and bare,
    You lean, and listen, and pulse, and throb;
The viols are dreaming between us two,
    And my gilded crown is no make-believe,
I am more than an actor, dear, to you,
    For you called me your king but yester eve,
And your heart is my golden coronet,
        Little Babette.

E. PAULINE JOHNSON

Low Tide at St. Andrews

(New Brunswick)

The long red flats stretch open to the sky,
Breathing their moisture on the August air.
The seaweeds cling with flesh-like fingers where
The rocks give shelter that the sands deny;
And wrapped in all her summer harmonies
St. Andrews sleeps beside her sleeping seas.

The far-off shores swim blue and indistinct,
Like half-lost memories of some old dream.
The listless waves that catch each sunny gleam
Are idling up the waterways land-linked,
And, yellowing along the harbor's breast,
The light is leaping shoreward from the west.

And naked-footed children, tripping down,
Light with young laughter, daily come at eve
To gather dulse and sea clams and then heave
Their loads, returning laden to the town,
Leaving a strange grey silence when they go,—
The silence of the sands when tides are low.

Beyond the Blue

Speak of you, sir? You bet he did. Ben Fields was far too sound
To go back on a fellow just because he weren't around.
Why, sir, he thought a lot of you, and only three months back
Says he, "The Squire will sometime come a-snuffing out our track
And give us the surprise." And so I got to thinking then
That any day you might drop down on Rove, and me, and Ben.
And now you've come for nothing, for the lad has left us two,
And six long weeks ago, sir, he went up beyond the blue.

Who's Rove? Oh, he's the collie, and the only thing on earth
That I will ever love again. Why, Squire, that dog is worth
More than you ever handled, and that's quite a piece, I know.
Ah, there the beggar is!—come here, you scalawag! and show
Your broken leg all bandaged up. Yes, sir, it's pretty sore;
I did it,—curse me,—and I think I feel the pain far more
Than him, for somehow I just feel as if I'd been untrue
To what my brother said before he went beyond the blue.

You see, the day before he died he says to me, "Say, Ned,
Be sure you take good care of poor old Rover when I'm dead,
And maybe he will cheer your lonesome hours up a bit,
And when he takes to you just see that you're deserving it."
Well, Squire, it wasn't any use. I tried, but couldn't get
The friendship of that collie, for I needed it, you bet.
I might as well have tried to get the moon to help me through,
For Rover's heart had gone with Ben, 'way up beyond the blue.

He never seemed to take to me nor follow me about,
For all I coaxed and petted, for my heart was starving out
For want of some companionship,—I thought, if only he
Would lick my hand or come and put his head aside my knee,
Perhaps his touch would scatter something of the gloom away.
But all alone I had to live until there came a day
When, tired of the battle, as you'd have tired too,
I wished to heaven I'd gone with Ben, 'way up beyond the blue.
  *   *   *   *   *   *   *   *   *   *

E. PAULINE JOHNSON

One morning I took out Ben's gun, and thought I'd hunt all day,
And started through the clearing for the bush that forward lay,
When something made me look around—I scarce believed my mind—
But, sure enough, the dog was following right close behind.
A feeling first of joy, and then a sharper, greater one
Of anger came, at knowing 'twas not me, but Ben's old gun,
That Rove was after,—well, sir, I just don't mind telling you,
But I forgot that moment Ben was up beyond the blue.

Perhaps it was but jealousy—perhaps it was despair,—
But I just struck him with the gun and broke the bone right there;
And then—my very throat seemed choked, for he began to whine
With pain—God knows how tenderly I took that dog of mine
Up in my arms, and tore my old red necktie into bands
To bind the broken leg, while there he lay and licked my hands;
And though I cursed my soul, it was the brightest day I knew,
Or even cared to live, since Ben went up beyond the blue.

I tell you, Squire, I nursed him just as gently as could be,
And now I'm all the world to him, and he's the world to me.
Look, sir, at that big, noble soul, right in his faithful eyes,
The square, forgiving honesty that deep down in them lies.
Eh, Squire? What's that you say? *He's got no soul?* I tell you, then,
He's grander and he's better than the mass of what's called men;
And I guess he stands a better chance than many of us do
Of seeing Ben some day again, 'way up beyond the blue.

The Mariner

"Wreck and stray and castaway."

—Swinburne

Once more adrift.
O'er dappling sea and broad lagoon,
O'er frowning cliff and yellow dune,
The long, warm lights of afternoon
    Like jewel dustings sift.

Once more awake.
I dreamed an hour of port and quay,
Of anchorage not meant for me;
The sea, the sea, the hungry sea
    Came rolling up the break.

Once more afloat.
The billows on my moorings press't,
They drove me from my moment's rest,
And now a portless sea I breast,
    And shelterless my boat.

Once more away.
The harbor lights are growing dim,
The shore is but a purple rim,
The sea outstretches gray and grim,
    Away, away, away!

Once more at sea,
The old, old sea I used to sail,
The battling tide, the blowing gale,
The waves with ceaseless under-wail,
    The life that used to be.

E. PAULINE JOHNSON

LULLABY OF THE IROQUOIS

Little brown baby-bird, lapped in your nest,
 Wrapped in your nest,
 Strapped in your nest,
Your straight little cradle-board rocks you to rest;
 Its hands are your nest,
 Its bands are your nest;
It swings from the down-bending branch of the oak;
You watch the camp flame, and the curling gray smoke;
But, oh, for your pretty black eyes sleep is best,—
Little brown baby of mine, go to rest.

Little brown baby-bird swinging to sleep,
 Winging to sleep,
 Singing to sleep,
Your wonder-black eyes that so wide open keep,
 Shielding their sleep,
 Unyielding to sleep,
The heron is homing, the plover is still,
The night-owl calls from his haunt on the hill,
Afar the fox barks, afar the stars peep,—
Little brown baby of mine, go to sleep.

The Corn Husker

Hard by the Indian lodges, where the bush
    Breaks in a clearing, through ill-fashioned fields,
She comes to labor, when the first still hush
    Of autumn follows large and recent yields.

Age in her fingers, hunger in her face,
    Her shoulders stooped with weight of work and years,
But rich in tawny coloring of her race,
    She comes a-field to strip the purple ears.

And all her thoughts are with the days gone by,
    Ere might's injustice banished from their lands
Her people, that today unheeded lie,
    Like the dead husks that rustle through her hands.

E. PAULINE JOHNSON

Prairie Greyhounds

C. P. R. "No. 1," Westbound

I swing to the sunset land—
The world of prairie, the world of plain,
The world of promise and hope and gain,
The world of gold, and the world of grain,
    And the world of the willing hand.

I carry the brave and bold—
The one who works for the nation's bread,
The one whose past is a thing that's dead,
The one who battles and beats ahead,
    And the one who goes for gold.

I swing to the "Land to Be,"
I am the power that laid its floors,
I am the guide to its western stores,
I am the key to its golden doors,
    That open alone to me.

C. P. R. "No. 2," Eastbound

I swing to the land of morn;
The grey old east with its grey old seas,
The land of leisure, the land of ease,
The land of flowers and fruits and trees,
    And the place where we were born.

Freighted with wealth I come;
For he who many a moon has spent
Far out west on adventure bent,
With well-worn pick and a folded tent,
    Is bringing his bullion home.

I never will be renowned,
As my twin that swings to the western marts,
For I am she of the humbler parts,
But I am the joy of the waiting hearts;
For I am the Homeward-bound.

E. PAULINE JOHNSON

GOLDEN—OF THE SELKIRKS

A trail upwinds from Golden;
It leads to a land God only knows,
To the land of eternal frozen snows,
That trail unknown and olden.

And they tell a tale that is strange and wild—
Of a lovely and lonely mountain child
That went up the trail from Golden.

A child in the sweet of her womanhood,
Beautiful, tender, grave and good
As the saints in time long olden.

And the days count not, nor the weeks avail;
For the child that went up the mountain trail
Came never again to Golden.

And the watchers wept in the midnight gloom,
Where the cañons yawn and the Selkirks loom,
For the love that they knew of olden.

And April dawned, with its suns aflame,
And the eagles wheeled and the vultures came
And poised o'er the town of Golden.

God of the white eternal peaks,
Guard the dead while the vulture seeks!—
God of the days so olden.

For only God in His greatness knows
Where the mountain holly above her grows,
On the trail that leads from Golden.

THE SONGSTER

Music, music with throb and swing,
    Of a plaintive note, and long;
'Tis a note no human throat could sing,
No harp with its dulcet golden string,—
Nor lute, nor lyre with liquid ring,
    Is sweet as the robin's song.

He sings for love of the season
    When the days grow warm and long,
For the beautiful God-sent reason
    That his breast was born for song.

Calling, calling so fresh and clear,
    Through the song-sweet days of May;
Warbling there, and whistling here,
He swells his voice on the drinking ear,
On the great, wide, pulsing atmosphere
    Till his music drowns the day.

He sings for love of the season
    When the days grow warm and long,
For the beautiful God-sent reason
    That his breast was born for song.

E. PAULINE JOHNSON

Thistle-Down

Beyond a ridge of pine with russet tips
The west lifts to the sun her longing lips,

Her blushes stain with gold and garnet dye
The shore, the river, and the wide far sky;

Like floods of wine the waters filter through
The reeds that brush our indolent canoe.

I beach the bow where sands in shadows lie;
You hold my hand a space, then speak goodbye.

Upwinds your pathway through the yellow plumes
Of goldenrod, profuse in August blooms,

And o'er its tossing sprays you toss a kiss;
A moment more, and I see only this—

The idle paddle you so lately held,
The empty bow your pliant wrist propelled,

Some thistles purpling into violet,
Their blossoms with a thousand thorns afret,

And like a cobweb, shadowy and gray,
Far floats their down—far drifts my dream away.

The Riders of the Plains*

Who is it lacks the knowledge? Who are the curs that dare
To whine and sneer that they do not fear the whelps in the Lion's lair?
But we of the North will answer, while life in the North remains,
Let the curs beware lest the whelps they dare are the Riders of the
    Plains;
For these are the kind whose muscle makes the power of the Lion's
    jaw,
And they keep the peace of our people and the honor of British law.

A woman has painted a picture,—'tis a neat little bit of art
The critics aver, and it roused up for her the love of the big British
    heart.
'Tis a sketch of an English bulldog that tigers would scarce attack,
And round and about and beneath him is painted the Union Jack,
With its blaze of color, and courage, its daring in every fold,
And underneath is the title, "What we have we'll hold."
'Tis a picture plain as a mirror, but the reflex it contains
Is the counterpart of the life and heart of the Riders of the Plains;
For like to that flag and that motto, and the power of that bulldog's
    jaw,
They keep the peace of our people and the honor of British law.

These are the fearless fighters, whose life in the open lies,
Who never fail on the prairie trail 'neath the Territorial skies,
Who have laughed in the face of the bullets and the edge of the rebels'
    steel,
Who have set their ban on the lawless man with his crime beneath
    their heel;
These are the men who battle the blizzards, the suns, the rains,

---

* Note.—The above is the territorial pet name for the Northwest Mounted Police, and is in general usage throughout Assiniboia, Saskatchewan and Alberta. At a dinner party in Boston the writer was asked, "Who are the Northwest Mounted Police?" and when told that they were the pride of Canada's fighting men the questioner sneered and replied, "Ah! then they are only some of your British Lion's whelps. *We are not afraid of them.*" His companions applauded the remark.

E. PAULINE JOHNSON

These are the famed that the North has named the "Riders of the
    Plains,"
And theirs is the might and the meaning and the strength of the
    bulldog's jaw,
While they keep the peace of the people and the honor of British law.

These are the men of action, who need not the world's renown,
For their valor is known to England's throne as a gem in the British
    crown;
These are the men who face the front, whose courage the world may
    scan,
The men who are feared by the felon, but are loved by the honest man;
These are the marrow, the pith, the cream, the best that the blood
    contains,
Who have cast their days in the valiant ways of the Riders of the
    Plains;
And theirs is the kind whose muscle makes the power of old
    England's jaw,
And they keep the peace of her people and the honor of British law.

Then down with the cur that questions,—let him sink to his craven
    den,—
For he daren't deny our hot reply as to "who are our mounted men."
He shall honor them east and westward, he shall honor them south
    and north,
He shall bare his head to that coat of red wherever that red rides forth.
'Tis well that he knows the fibre that the great Northwest contains,
The Northwest pride in her men that ride on the Territorial plains,—
For of such as these are the muscles and the teeth in the Lion's jaw,
And they keep the peace of our people and the honor of British law.

SILHOUETTE

The sky-line melts from russet into blue,
Unbroken the horizon, saving where
A wreath of smoke curls up the far, thin air,
And points the distant lodges of the Sioux.

Etched where the lands and cloudlands touch and die
A solitary Indian tepee stands,
The only habitation of these lands,
That roll their magnitude from sky to sky.

The tent poles lift and loom in thin relief,
The upward floating smoke ascends between,
And near the open doorway, gaunt and lean,
And shadow-like, there stands an Indian Chief.

With eyes that lost their lustre long ago,
With visage fixed and stern as fate's decree,
He looks towards the empty west, to see
The never-coming herd of buffalo.

Only the bones that bleach upon the plains,
Only the fleshless skeletons that lie
In ghastly nakedness and silence, cry
Out mutely that nought else to him remains.

A Prodigal

My heart forgot its God for love of you,
    And you forgot me, other loves to learn;
Now through a wilderness of thorn and rue
    Back to my God I turn.

And just because my God forgets the past,
    And in forgetting does not ask to know
Why I once left His arms for yours, at last
    Back to my God I go.

"Through Time and Bitter Distance"*

Unknown to you, I walk the cheerless shore.
    The cutting blast, the hurl of biting brine
May freeze, and still, and bind the waves at war,
    Ere you will ever know, O! Heart of mine,
That I have sought, reflected in the blue
    Of those sea depths, some shadow of your eyes;
Have hoped the laughing waves would sing of you,
    But this is all my starving sight descries—

I

Far out at sea a sail
    Bends to the freshening breeze,
Yields to the rising gale
    That sweeps the seas;

II

Yields, as a bird wind-tossed,
    To saltish waves that fling
Their spray, whose rime and frost
    Like crystals cling

III

To canvas, mast and spar,
    Till, gleaming like a gem,
She sinks beyond the far
    Horizon's hem,

---

* For this title the author is indebted to Mr. Charles G. D. Roberts. It occurs in his sonnet, "Rain."

E. PAULINE JOHNSON

IV

Lost to my longing sight,
    And nothing left to me
Save an oncoming night,—
    An empty sea.

At Half-mast

You didn't know Billy, did you? Well, Bill was one of the boys,
The greatest fellow you ever seen to racket an' raise a noise,—
An' sing! say, you never heard singin' 'nless you heard Billy sing.
I used to say to him, "Billy, that voice that you've got there 'd bring
A mighty sight more bank-notes to tuck away in your vest,
If only you'd go on the concert stage instead of a-ranchin' West."
An' Billy he'd jist go laughin', and say as I didn't know
A robin's whistle in springtime from a barnyard rooster's crow.
But Billy could sing, an' I sometimes think that voice lives anyhow,—
That perhaps Bill helps with the music in the place he's gone to now.

The last time that I seen him was the day he rode away;
He was goin' acrost the plain to catch the train for the East next day.
'Twas the only time I ever seen poor Bill that he didn't laugh
Or sing, an' kick up a rumpus an' racket around, and chaff,
For he'd got a letter from his folks that said for to hurry home,
For his mother was dyin' away down East and she wanted Bill to come.
Say, but the feller took it hard, but he saddled up right away,
An' started across the plains to take the train for the East, next day.
Sometimes I lie awake a-nights jist a-thinkin' of the rest,
For that was the great big blizzard day, when the wind come down
    from west,

An' the snow piled up like mountains an' we couldn't put foot outside,
But jist set into the shack an' talked of Bill on his lonely ride.
We talked of the laugh he threw us as he went at the break o' day,
An' we talked of the poor old woman dyin' a thousand mile away.

Well, Dan O'Connell an' I went out to search at the end of the week,
Fer all of us fellers thought a lot,—a lot that we darsn't speak.
We'd been up the trail about forty mile, an' was talkin' of turnin' back,
But Dan, well, he wouldn't give in, so we kep' right on to the railroad
    track.
As soon as we sighted them telegraph wires says Dan, "Say, bless my
    soul!
Ain't that there Bill's red handkerchief tied half way up that pole?"

E. PAULINE JOHNSON

Yes, sir, there she was, with her ends a-flippin' an' flyin' in the wind,
An' underneath was the envelope of Bill's letter tightly pinned.
"Why, he must a-boarded the train right here," says Dan, but I kinder
    knew
That underneath them snowdrifts we would find a thing or two;
Fer he'd writ on that there paper, "Been lost fer hours,—all hope is
    past.
You'll find me, boys, where my handkerchief is flyin' at half-mast."

THE SLEEPING GIANT

(Thunder Bay, Lake Superior)

When did you sink to your dreamless sleep
    Out there in your thunder bed?
Where the tempests sweep,
And the waters leap,
    And the storms rage overhead.

Were you lying there on your couch alone
    Ere Egypt and Rome were born?
Ere the Age of Stone,
Or the world had known
    The Man with the Crown of Thorn.

The winds screech down from the open west,
    And the thunders beat and break
On the amethyst
Of your rugged breast,—
    But you never arise or wake.

You have locked your past, and you keep the key
    In your heart 'neath the westing sun,
Where the mighty sea
And its shores will be
    Storm-swept till the world is done.

The Quill Worker

Plains, plains, and the prairie land which the sunlight floods and fills,
To the north the open country, southward the Cypress Hills;
Never a bit of woodland, never a rill that flows,
Only a stretch of cactus beds, and the wild, sweet prairie rose;
Never a habitation, save where in the far southwest
A solitary tepee lifts its solitary crest,
Where Neykia in the doorway, crouched in the red sunshine,
Broiders her buckskin mantle with the quills of the porcupine.

Neykia, the Sioux chief's daughter, she with the foot that flies,
She with the hair of midnight and the wondrous midnight eyes,
She with the deft brown fingers, she with the soft, slow smile,
She with the voice of velvet and the thoughts that dream the while,—
"Whence come the vague tomorrows? Where do the yesters fly?
What is beyond the border of the prairie and the sky?
Does the maid in the Land of Morning sit in the red sunshine,
Broidering her buckskin mantle with the quills of the porcupine?"

So Neykia, in the westland, wonders and works away,
Far from the fret and folly of the "Land of Waking Day."
And many the pale-face trader who stops at the tepee door
For a smile from the sweet, shy worker, and a sigh when the hour is
    o'er.
For they know of a young red hunter who oftentimes has stayed
To rest and smoke with her father, tho' his eyes were on the maid;
And the moons will not be many ere she in the red sunshine
Will broider his buckskin mantle with the quills of the porcupine.

GUARD OF THE EASTERN GATE

Halifax sits on her hills by the sea
    In the might of her pride,—
Invincible, terrible, beautiful, she
    With a sword at her side.

To right and to left of her, battlements rear
    And fortresses frown;
While she sits on her throne without favor or fear,
    With her cannon as crown.

Coast guard and sentinel, watch of the weal
    Of a nation she keeps;
But her hand is encased in a gauntlet of steel,
    And her thunder but sleeps.

E. PAULINE JOHNSON

AT CROW'S NEST PASS

At Crow's Nest Pass the mountains rend
Themselves apart, the rivers wend
    A lawless course about their feet,
    And breaking into torrents beat
In useless fury where they blend
        At Crow's Nest Pass.

The nesting eagle, wise, discreet,
Wings up the gorge's lone retreat
And makes some barren crag her friend
        At Crow's Nest Pass.

Uncertain clouds, half-high, suspend
Their shifting vapors, and contend
    With rocks that suffer not defeat;
    And snows, and suns, and mad winds meet
To battle where the cliffs defend
        At Crow's Nest Pass.

"Give Us Barabbas"*

There was a man—a Jew of kingly blood,
　　But of the people—poor and lowly born,
Accused of blasphemy of God, he stood
　　Before the Roman Pilate, while in scorn
The multitude demanded it was fit
　　That one should suffer for the people, while
Another be released, absolved, acquit,
　　To live his life out virtuous or vile.

"Whom will ye have—Barabbas or this Jew?"
　　Pilate made answer to the mob, "The choice
Is yours; I wash my hands of this, and you,
　　Do as you will." With one vast ribald voice
The populace arose and, shrieking, cried,
　　"Give us Barabbas, we condone his deeds!"
And He of Nazareth was crucified—
　　Misjudged, condemned, dishonored for their needs.

And down these nineteen centuries anew
　　Comes the hoarse-throated, brutalized refrain,
"Give us Barabbas, crucify the Jew!"
　　Once more a man must bear a nation's stain,—
And that in France, the chivalrous, whose lore
　　Made her the flower of knightly age gone by.
Now she lies hideous with a leprous sore
　　No skill can cure—no pardon purify.

And an indignant world, transfixed with hate
　　Of such disease, cries, as in Herod's time,
Pointing its finger at her festering state,
　　"Room for the leper, and her leprous crime!"
And France, writhing from years of torment, cries
　　Out in her anguish, "Let this Jew endure,

---

* NOTE.—Written after Dreyfus was exiled.

Damned and disgraced, vicarious sacrifice.
   The honor of my army is secure."

And, vampire-like, that army sucks the blood
   From out a martyr's veins, and strips his crown
Of honor from him, and his herohood
   Flings in the dust, and cuts his manhood down.
Hide from your God, O! ye that did this act!
   With lesser crimes the halls of Hell are paved.
Your army's honor may be still intact,
   Unstained, unsoiled, unspotted,—but unsaved.

Your Mirror Frame

Methinks I see your mirror frame,
　　Ornate with photographs of them.
Place mine therein, for, all the same,
　　I'll have my little laughs at them.

For girls may come, and girls may go,
　　I think I have the best of them;
And yet this photograph I know
　　You'll toss among the rest of them.

I cannot even hope that you
　　Will put me in your locket, dear;
Nor costly frame will I look through,
　　Nor bide in your breast pocket, dear.

For none your heart monopolize,
　　You favor such a nest of them.
So I but hope your roving eyes
　　Seek mine among the rest of them.

For saucy sprite, and noble dame,
　　And many a dainty maid of them
Will greet me in your mirror frame,
　　And share your kisses laid on them.

And yet, sometimes I fancy, dear,
　　You hold me as the best of them.
So I'm content if I appear
　　Tonight with all the rest of them.

The City and the Sea

I

To none the city bends a servile knee;
 Purse-proud and scornful, on her heights she stands,
And at her feet the great white moaning sea
 Shoulders incessantly the grey-gold sands,—
One the Almighty's child since time began,
 And one the might of Mammon, born of clods;
For all the city is the work of man,
 But all the sea is God's.

II

And she—between the ocean and the town—
 Lies cursed of one and by the other blest;
Her staring eyes, her long drenched hair, her gown,
 Sea-laved and soiled and dank above her breast.
She, image of her God since life began,
 She, but the child of Mammon, born of clods,
Her broken body spoiled and spurned of man,
 But her sweet soul is God's.

Fire-Flowers

And only where the forest fires have sped,
    Scorching relentlessly the cool north lands,
A sweet wild flower lifts its purple head,
And, like some gentle spirit sorrow-fed,
    It hides the scars with almost human hands.

And only to the heart that knows of grief,
    Of desolating fire, of human pain,
There comes some purifying sweet belief,
Some fellow-feeling beautiful, if brief,
    And life revives, and blossoms once again.

A Toast

There's wine in the cup, Vancouver,
    And there's warmth in my heart for you,
While I drink to your health, your youth, and your wealth,
    And the things that you yet will do.
In a vintage rare and olden,
    With a flavor fine and keen,
Fill the glass to the edge, while I stand up to pledge
    My faith to my western queen.

Then here's a Ho! Vancouver, in wine of the bonniest hue,
    With a hand on my hip and the cup at my lip,
And a love in my life for you.
    For you are a jolly good fellow, with a great, big heart, I know;
So I drink this toast
To the "Queen of the Coast."
    Vancouver, here's a Ho!

And here's to the days that are coming,
    And here's to the days that are gone,
And here's to your gold and your spirit bold,
    And your luck that has held its own;
And here's to your hands so sturdy,
    And here's to your hearts so true,
And here's to the speed of the day decreed
    That brings me again to you.

Then here's a Ho! Vancouver, in wine of the bonniest hue,
    With a hand on my hip and the cup at my lip,
And a love in my life for you.
    For you are a jolly good fellow, with a great, big heart, I know;
So I drink this toast
To the "Queen of the Coast."
    Vancouver, here's a Ho!

LADY ICICLE

Little Lady Icicle is dreaming in the north-land
And gleaming in the north-land, her pillow all a-glow;
    For the frost has come and found her
    With an ermine robe around her
Where little Lady Icicle lies dreaming in the snow.

Little Lady Icicle is waking in the north-land,
And shaking in the north-land her pillow to and fro;
    And the hurricane a-skirling
    Sends the feathers all a-whirling
Where little Lady Icicle is waking in the snow.

Little Lady Icicle is laughing in the north-land,
And quaffing in the north-land her wines that overflow;
    All the lakes and rivers crusting
    That her finger-tips are dusting,
Where little Lady Icicle is laughing in the snow.

Little Lady Icicle is singing in the north-land,
And bringing from the north-land a music wild and low;
    And the fairies watch and listen
    Where her silver slippers glisten,
As little Lady Icicle goes singing through the snow.

Little Lady Icicle is coming from the north-land,
Benumbing all the north-land where'er her feet may go;
    With a fringe of frost before her
    And a crystal garment o'er her,
Little Lady Icicle is coming with the snow.

The Legend of Qu'Appelle Valley

I am the one who loved her as my life,
    Had watched her grow to sweet young womanhood;
Won the dear privilege to call her wife,
    And found the world, because of her, was good.
I am the one who heard the spirit voice,
    Of which the paleface settlers love to tell;
From whose strange story they have made their choice
    Of naming this fair valley the "Qu'Appelle."

She had said fondly in my eager ear—
    "When Indian summer smiles with dusky lip,
Come to the lakes, I will be first to hear
    The welcome music of thy paddle dip.
I will be first to lay in thine my hand,
    To whisper words of greeting on the shore;
And when thou would'st return to thine own land,
    I'll go with thee, thy wife for evermore."

Not yet a leaf had fallen, not a tone
    Of frost upon the plain ere I set forth,
Impatient to possess her as my own—
    This queen of all the women of the North.
I rested not at even or at dawn,
    But journeyed all the dark and daylight through—
Until I reached the Lakes, and, hurrying on,
    I launched upon their bosom my canoe.

Of sleep or hunger then I took no heed,
    But hastened o'er their leagues of waterways;
But my hot heart outstripped my paddle's speed
    And waited not for distance or for days,
But flew before me swifter than the blade
    Of magic paddle ever cleaved the Lake,
Eager to lay its love before the maid,
    And watch the lovelight in her eyes awake.

So the long days went slowly drifting past;
    It seemed that half my life must intervene
Before the morrow, when I said at last—
    "One more day's journey and I win my queen!"
I rested then, and, drifting, dreamed the more
    Of all the happiness I was to claim,—
When suddenly from out the shadowed shore,
    I heard a voice speak tenderly my name.

"Who calls?" I answered; no reply; and long
    I stilled my paddle blade and listened. Then
Above the night wind's melancholy song
    I heard distinctly that strange voice again—
A woman's voice, that through the twilight came
    Like to a soul unborn—a song unsung.
I leaned and listened—yes, she spoke my name,
    And then I answered in the quaint French tongue,

"Qu'Appelle? Qu'Appelle?" No answer, and the night
    Seemed stiller for the sound, till round me fell
The far-off echoes from the far-off height—
    "Qu'Appelle?" my voice came back, "Qu'Appelle? Qu'Appelle?"
This—and no more; I called aloud until
    I shuddered as the gloom of night increased,
And, like a pallid spectre wan and chill,
    The moon arose in silence from the east.

I dare not linger on the moment when
    My boat I beached beside her tepee door;
I heard the wail of women and of men,—
    I saw the death-fires lighted on the shore.
No language tells the torture or the pain,
    The bitterness that flooded all my life,—
When I was led to look on her again,
    That queen of women pledged to be my wife.

To look upon the beauty of her face,
    The still closed eyes, the lips that knew no breath;

To look, to learn,—to realize my place
    Had been usurped by my one rival—Death.
A storm of wrecking sorrow beat and broke
    About my heart, and life shut out its light
Till through my anguish someone gently spoke,
    And said, "Twice did she call for thee last night."
I started up—and bending o'er my dead,
    Asked when did her sweet lips in silence close.
"She called thy name—then passed away," they said,
    "Just on the hour whereat the moon arose."

Among the lonely lakes I go no more,
    For she who made their beauty is not there;
The paleface rears his tepee on the shore
    And says the vale is fairest of the fair.
Full many years have vanished since, but still
    The voyageurs beside the campfire tell
How, when the moonrise tips the distant hill,
    They hear strange voices through the silence swell.
The paleface loves the haunted lakes they say,
    And journeys far to watch their beauty spread
Before his vision; but to me the day,
    The night, the hour, the seasons all are dead.
I listen heartsick, while the hunters tell
    Why white men named the valley The Qu'Appelle.

The Art of Alma-Tadema

There is no song his colors cannot sing,
    For all his art breathes melody, and tunes
The fine, keen beauty that his brushes bring
    To murmuring marbles and to golden Junes.

The music of those marbles you can hear
    In every crevice, where the deep green stains
Have sunken when the grey days of the year
    Spilled leisurely their warm, incessant rains

That, lingering, forgot to leave the ledge,
    But drenched into the seams, amid the hush
Of ages, leaving but the silent pledge
    To waken to the wonder of his brush.

And at the Master's touch the marbles leap
    To life, the creamy onyx and the skins
Of copper-colored leopards, and the deep,
    Cool basins where the whispering water wins

Reflections from the gold and glowing sun,
    And tints from warm, sweet human flesh, for fair
And subtly lithe and beautiful, leans one—
    A goddess with a wealth of tawny hair.

Goodbye

Sounds of the seas grow fainter,
    Sounds of the sands have sped;
The sweep of gales,
The far white sails,
    Are silent, spent and dead.

Sounds of the days of summer
    Murmur and die away,
And distance hides
The long, low tides,
    As night shuts out the day.

A Note About the Author

E. Pauline Johnson (1861–1913) was a Canadian poet and actress. Also known by her stage name Tekahionwake, Johnson was born to an English mother and a Mohawk father in Six Nations, Ontario. Johnson suffered from illness as a child, keeping her from school and encouraging her self-education through the works of Longfellow, Tennyson, Browning, Byron, and Keats. Despite the racism suffered by Canada's indigenous people, Johnson was encouraged to learn about her Mohawk heritage, much of which came from her paternal grandfather John Smoke Johnson, who shared with her and her siblings his knowledge of the oral tradition of their people. In the 1880s, Johnson began acting and writing for small theater productions, finding success in 1892 with a popular solo act emphasizing her duel heritage. In these performances, Johnson would wear both indigenous and Victorian English costumes, reciting original poetry for each persona. As a poet, she wrote prolifically for such periodicals as *Globe* and *Saturday Night*, publishing her first collection, *The White Wampum*, in 1895. Her death at the age of 52 prompted an outpouring of grief and celebration in Canada; at the time, Johnson's funeral was the largest in Vancouver history, attracting thousands of mourners from all walks of life.

A Note from the Publisher

Spanning many genres, from non-fiction essays to literature classics to children's books and lyric poetry, Mint Edition books showcase the master works of our time in a modern new package. The text is freshly typeset, is clean and easy to read, and features a new note about the author in each volume. Many books also include exclusive new introductory material. Every book boasts a striking new cover, which makes it as appropriate for collecting as it is for gift giving. Mint Edition books are only printed when a reader orders them, so natural resources are not wasted. We're proud that our books are never manufactured in excess and exist only in the exact quantity they need to be read and enjoyed.

bookfinity™

Discover more of your favorite classics with Bookfinity™.

- Track your reading with custom book lists.
- Get great book recommendations for your personalized Reader Type.
- Add reviews for your favorite books.
- AND MUCH MORE!

Visit **bookfinity.com** and take the fun Reader Type quiz to get started.

Enjoy our classic and modern companion pairings!

Classic & Modern